D1460410

FOR A

Fabulous

WIFE

summersdale

FOR A FABULOUS WIFE

Summersdale Publishers Ltd
46 West Street
Chichester
West Sussex
PO19 1RP
UK

www.summersdale.com

Printed and bound in China.

ISBN: 978-1-84953-290-7

Substantial discounts on bulk quantities of Summersdale books are available to corporations, professional associations and other organisations. For details contact Summersdale Publishers by telephone: +44 (0) 1243 771107, fax: +44 (0) 1243 786300 or email: nicky@summersdale.com.

To.....................................

From.....................................

My most brilliant achievement was my ability to be able to persuade my wife to marry me.

WINSTON CHURCHILL

You are my heart, my life,
my one and only thought.

SIR AATHUA CONAN DOYLE

Every man who is high up likes to think that he has done it all himself, and the wife smiles and lets it go at that.

J. M. BARRIE

A study revealed that 27 per cent of husbands had bought their wives clothes or underwear in the wrong size. None of them admitted it had been wishful thinking.

In my house I'm the boss, my wife is just the decision maker.

WOODY ALLEN

You're fabulous because...

... you know how to keep
the romance going.

Don't marry the person you think you can live with; marry only the individual you think you can't live without.

DR JAMES C. DOBSON

The best thing to hold onto in life is each other.

AUDREY HEPBURN

You deserve
an award for:

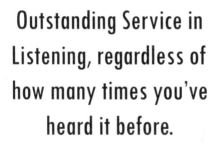

Outstanding Service in Listening, regardless of how many times you've heard it before.

Affection is responsible for nine-tenths of whatever solid and durable happiness there is in our lives.

C. S. LEWIS

A kiss makes the heart young again and wipes out the years.

RUPERT BROOKE

Kissing for just one minute burns a total of 26 calories… If we kiss for three and a half minutes, that's worth a chocolate digestive!

Let us now set forth one of the fundamental truths about marriage: the wife is in charge.

BILL COSBY

You're
fabulous
because...

... you know how to
keep Mum happy

Marriage is a mistake every man should make.

GEORGE JESSEL

Cooking is like love. It should be entered into with abandon or not at all.

HARRIET VAN HORNE

My husband says I feed him like he's a god: every meal is a burnt offering.

AHONDA HANSOME

*You deserve
an award for:*

Most Persuasive
Argument when
convincing me not to
wear something dreadful.

Love can turn the cottage into a golden palace.

GERMAN PROVERB

Of all the home remedies,
a good wife is best.

KIN HUBBARD

A psychiatrist asks
a lot of expensive
questions your wife
asks for nothing.

JOEY ADAMS

Happy is the man who finds a true friend, and far happier is he who finds that true friend in his wife.

FRANZ SCHUBERT

Marriage, n. A community consisting of a master, a mistress, and two slaves, making in all two.

AMBROSE BIERCE, THE DEVIL'S DICTIONARY

You're fabulous because...

... you pretend to be interested when I talk about my boring day.

'Tis strange what a man may do, and a woman yet think him an angel.

WILLIAM MAKEPEACE THACKERAY

Two souls with but
a single thought,
Two hearts that
beat as one.

JOHN KEATS

You deserve an award for:

Heroic Patience while watching the film I wanted to see.

A successful marriage requires falling in love many times, always with the same person.

MIGNON MCLAUGHLIN

We are not the same persons this year as last; nor are those we love. It is a happy chance if we, changing, continue to love a changed person.

W. SOMERSET MAUGHAM

Researchers say that falling in love can induce a calming effect and can raise levels of nerve growth factor, improving your memory — but only for the first year.

Marriage is the alliance of two people, one of whom never remembers birthdays and the other never forgets them.

OGDEN NASH

You're fabulous because...

... you remember all the things I forget (including where I left my keys).

The best way to
remember your
wife's birthday is
to forget it once.

E. JOSEPH COSSMAN

Happy is a man with a wife to tell him what to do and a secretary to do it.

STORMONT MANCROFT

The husband who decides to surprise his wife is often very much surprised himself.

VOLTAIRE

*You deserve
an award for:*

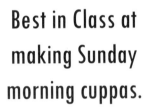

Best in Class at making Sunday morning cuppas.

Heaven will be no heaven to me if I do not meet my wife there.

ANDREW JACKSON

Your words are my food,
your breath my wine. You
are everything to me.

SARAH BERNHARDT

Nothing flatters a man as much as the happiness of his wife.

SAMUEL JOHNSON

In a poll, 62 per cent of married people said that sharing of housework was the key ingredient of a successful marriage.

I judge how much a man cares for a woman by the space he allots her under a jointly shared umbrella.

JIMMY CANNON

You're fabulous because...

... you know how to do things
I have no clue about.

There is a woman
at the beginning of
all great things.

ALPHONSE DE LAMARTINE

Being deeply loved by someone gives you strength, while loving someone deeply gives you courage.

LAO TZU

You deserve an award for:

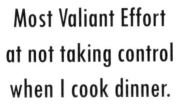

Most Valiant Effort
at not taking control
when I cook dinner.

In a husband there is only a man; in a married woman there is a man, a father and mother, and a woman.

HONORÉ DE BALZAC

She's adorned
Amply that in her
husband's eye
looks lovely.

JOHN TOBIN, THE HONEYMOON

Fascinating Fact

The ancient Greeks
believed the left ring
finger contained a
vein that ran straight
to the heart; 'the
vein of love'.

*There is nothing nobler
or more admirable
than when two people
who see eye to eye
keep house as man and
wife, confounding their
enemies and delighting
their friends.*

HOMER

You're fabulous because...

... you're always ready
to help me out.

All women should know how to take care of children. Most of them will have a husband some day.

FRANKLIN P. JONES

I chose my wife, as she did her wedding gown, not for a fine glossy surface, but such qualities as would wear well.

OLIVER GOLDSMITH, THE VICAR OF WAKEFIELD

A woman is like a teabag. It's only when she's in hot water that you realise how strong she is.

NANCY REAGAN

*You deserve
an award for:*

Outstanding
Contribution to
Alternative Navigation
when map-reading.

*An ideal wife is one
who remains faithful
to you but tries to
be just as charming
as if she weren't.*

SACHA GUITRY

I have learned that only two things are necessary to keep one's wife happy. First, let her think she's having her own way. And second, let her have it.

LYNDON B. JOHNSON

And yet, by heaven, I think my love as rare As any she belied with false compare.

WILLIAM SHAKESPEARE, SONNET 130

Studies have found that a marriage has a better chance of being long and happy if the wife is at least 27 per cent smarter than her husband.

Being a woman is a
terribly difficult task,
since it consists principally
in dealing with men.

JOSEPH CONRAD

You're fabulous because...

... you always support
me when I need it.

Marriage resembles a pair of shears, so joined that they cannot be separated; often moving in opposite directions, yet always punishing any one who comes between them.

SYDNEY SMITH

Love conquers all things: let us too surrender to love.

VIRGIL

You deserve an award for:

Determination during the longest shopping trip ever without actually buying anything.

The reason husbands and wives do not understand each other is because they belong to different sexes.

DOROTHY DIX

Women are meant to be loved, not to be understood.

OSCAR WILDE

Marriage counsellors recommend kissing your partner for 20 seconds every day. (And try not to look at your watch.)

The ideal story is that of two people who go into love step by step, with a fluttered consciousness, like a pair of children venturing together into a dark room.

ROBERT LOUIS STEVENSON

You're fabulous because...

... you look ravishing
whatever you wear.

We come to love not by finding the perfect person, but by learning to see an imperfect person perfectly.

SAM KEEN

No woman is worth more than a fiver unless you're in love with her. Then she's worth all she costs you.

W. SOMERSET MAUGHAM

But he that is married
careth for the things that
are of the world, how he
may please his wife.

1 CORINTHIANS 7:33

You deserve an award for:

Best Dramatic Performance
when encountering
tiny spiders.

When two hearts are one, even the king cannot separate them.

TURKISH PROVERB

Between a man and his wife nothing ought to rule but love.

WILLIAM PENN

Daniel F. and Susan Brewer Bakeman of New York were married from 1772 to 1863, for a total of 91 years and 12 days — the longest marriage ever recorded!

Love is... born with the pleasure of looking at each other, it is fed with the necessity of seeing each other, it is concluded with the impossibility of separation.

JOSÉ MARTÍ

I love being married. It's so great to find that one special person you want to annoy for the rest of your life.

RITA RUDNER

You're fabulous because...

. . . we can make great
memories together.

*To love abundantly
is to live abundantly,
and to love forever
is to live forever.*

HENRY DRUMMOND

If you live to be a hundred, I want to live to be a hundred minus one day so I never have to live without you.

A. A. MILNE

You deserve an award for:

Appreciation of
even the smallest of
romantic gestures.

What a happy and
holy fashion it is that
those who love one
another should rest
on the same pillow.

NATHANIEL HAWTHORNE

You're
fabulous
because...

. . . you don't mind letting me
have control of the remote (well,
at least some of the time!)

If you're interested in finding out more about our gift books follow us on Twitter: **@Summersdale**

www.summersdale.com